PROLOGUE

I am **not** a money manager, investment advisor or stockbroker. I am a well versed, well educated private investor. I understand economics. I see what the Fed is up against. I understand interest rates. I have been around a long time. I received my MBA from Columbia in 1957.

In my opinion we are in the early stages of what may prove to be a serious recession. The fact that the general public is taking losses on their investments because of a lack of information and knowledge is not acceptable. It is a defect in the investment business.

I have developed, for my own use, a proprietary investment system. It is easy to use for most people. It does not have a lot of complexities. It is clearly outlined in this book. It can be used by any interested person. It is not perfect by any means. It does make investing easy and should prevent large losses by taking an investor out of a loosing position early.

It is here for the personal use of individual investors only.

Victor Weintraub

HOW TO

INVEST IN STOCKS

AND

AVOID LOSSES

IN A DIFICULT MARKET

BY

VICTOR WEINTRAUB

Published by

First Capitol Books
Scottsdale Arizona

https://firstcap.com

Library of Congress Control Number
2022918972
Print ISBN 0984986839
E Book ISBN 978-0-9849868-4-2

Disclaimer

Victor Weintraub is **not** an investment advisor, money manager, wealth manager, or securities advisor. He does not have any federal securities licenses. Victor Weintraub is a private investor. This book is based solely upon his opinions experience and personal knowledge. It does not endorse any investment system or security analysis system put forward by any other individual or organization. Victor Weintraub is not a stockbroker or securities dealer and is not affiliated with any. He does not manage other people's money for a fee and will not if asked.

The use of the information contained in this book is solely at your own risk. No warranties are suggested or offered. Any stocks or securities mentioned in this book are for illustration purposes only and not an offer to sell.

Victor Weintraub is the owner of a mortgage company. This company makes residential and commercial mortgages. This company is not involved in any way in the securities business. The company does not sell stocks or manage money for other people and is not an agent or a fiduciary for anybody.

DEDICATION

To

Carole

Lauren Mo Michelle

Molly Max Eliana

QUOTE

"It is better to be roughly right than precisely wrong."

John Maynard Keynes

TABLE OF CONTENTS

CHAPTER 1

STOCK MARKET LOSSES

You are reading this book because you lost a load of money in the stock market. That's your own fault not mine. You listen to all the experts and all the guys on television. You didn't know anything about investing in the stock market. They were on TV they sounded very smart you listened to what they said.

Maybe you have an investment advisor. Or a financial planner. They are supposed to know what they're doing that is the business that they are in. Well the truth is there are no experts. A lot of people present themselves as being very knowledgeable. They say and know everything about stocks investing and money and the economy all that kind of good stuff. When you get right down to it they don't know what they are doing. The guy who says he's a financial advisor used to be a cab driver or an English major or a plumber.

So it all comes down to the fact that you were making good money from your job and you wanted to invest it. Well you are just like the average Joe. You're good at your job. You make a good living. You have money left over that you want to put to work. Let big brother take care of my money.

That doesn't solve any problems. Actually it creates more problems for you. If you are just going to go with the flow and allow the so-called experts to take care of things you are going to have a disaster. That is what happened.

So what are we going to do about it? There is no magic. You cannot read this book and get your money back. That is not going to happen. Obviously you have to begin to do things differently.

So what is the answer? You're not going to become an expert yourself. Investing is not what you do. All the experts are not so expert. They don't seem to know much more than you do. What to do differently?

Maybe the answer is a different method of investing. Something straightforward and easy to understand. Not a lot of bells and whistles or complicated formulas. Going back to basics. You know the old rule. Buy low sell high. Not hard to understand. Not easy to implement.

The answer is that you need a plan. A different plan that does not depend upon the conventional wisdom and the mumbo-jumbo of the experts. There are no experts. There is a lot of mumbo-jumbo. It does not amount to diddle. You have to separate the erudite sounding talk from basic knowledge.

This book puts forward a totally different method of investing. We do not have armies of analysts who project company incomes and price-earnings ratios. We do not talk to management. We do not talk to other analysts.

We do something very different. We look at history. We listen to what the Fed tells us.. But most importantly we look at what the stock market has done. Is doing. And probably will continue to do.

What we do is really common sense. We are not married to the idea that the market always goes up. We are not married to the idea that given enough time the market will correct all errors. We know that we are dealing with a market that goes up and down. We know that everything does not get corrected in time. We know that there are stocks that are still selling below their price of 10 years ago.

Read on. This book is an iconoclast. It shatters the incorrect assumptions of the stock market industry of the past. It is simple and straightforward. You can do it all in an hour or so a week. As I said before nothing complex. No mumbo-jumbo. A lot of common sense. No bull.

CHAPTER 2

MY TRADING SYSTEM

The purpose of this book is two fold. It is to provide you with some understanding of what is going on in the American economy, the world economy and the stock and bond markets today. It is also to give you a new and different trading system. A system that is not based on the conventional wisdom which does not work. I guess you could call me an iconoclast. I am going to try to dispel the ideas that the conventional wisdom still works and we are forever in a high liquidity easy money economy.

For the past 14 years we have been primarily in

an easy money, low interest rate environment. During that time we have had a few interest rate increases and decreases. Small. For the most part during that period we have had high employment.

So here we are. We have had a combination of full employment, low interest rates and high liquidity. The liquidity which the Fed intended to stimulate the economy instead found its way into stock market prices. Then into home prices. We did get an improved economy but it took more low interest rates and expanded liquidity to get there than the Fed expected. We also weathered the Covid pandemic. Now the Fed has decided to change the game. The problems of the 2008 banking crisis are gone. The Covid pandemic is gone. But inflation is here. The result of prior Fed action.

The last time the Fed initiated an assault on inflation was in 1980. At that time the problem was only inflation. Today the situation is different. In addition to low interest rates we have gone through a period of greatly increase liquidity. The result of the Fed greatly expanding its holdings of federal debt. The Fed is now trying to alleviate both problems at the same time.

I expect interest rates to go up substantially. It is already happening. I expect liquidity to go down dramatically. A slow start. There has been talk in the media about the possibility of a soft landing. There is no such thing. The reality is that interest rates are going up. Liquidity is going down. The stock market is going down. Treasury bonds are going down in price as interest rates go up. THUD! Nothing soft is happening.

What this requires is a totally different approach to stock market investment and stock market trading. We are no longer in the world of the conventional wisdom. The market always goes up. You can expect a 6% to 10% return over time. This conventional approach does not work any more,

The purpose of this book is to give you some insight as to what is happening in the economy and what we can expect to happen to interest rates and to the stock market ahead. You cannot be complacent and assume that everything will work out in time. I expect that we will see a different world when it comes to corporate earnings. payments on bank deposits, price-to-earnings ratios on stocks and industry growth expectations. We are in a new world. Back to reality.

I will describe my trading system later in this book. It is based on economic truth and the history of what has happened in the past. My trading system is totally different from what you have heard from investment advisers, stock market media and your friendly market expert.

I do not believe that the market goes up forever. I know that it goes up and down. The direction and amplitude of the market is dependent upon company earnings. Stock earnings multipliers are dependent upon future earnings and interest rates. I live in a world of reality. I do not expect that time will correct all problems. There are stocks today that have never seen the high that they made 10 or 15 years ago.

CHAPTER 3

WHAT IS HAPPENING NOW

I am writing this book in September 2022. At this point in time we are in the beginning of a recession. Stock market performance is well down from the beginning of the year. You would expect that the financial media and their various guests, many investment advisors, who appear would be commenting about the weak down market and interest rates. This is not the case.

The Federal Reserve Board, the Fed, has been talking about high inflation and their intention to increase interest rates and reduce liquidity for many months. Although the specific actions of the Fed have been reported there has been little or no commentary about the impact of tight money and reduced liquidity on the stock market and the economy. It appears to me that the public is being misinformed or should I say not informed about what is happening in the economy.

People in general have large investments in stock and the stock market. They expect to get proper information from the media. They expect to get guidance from their investment advisors.

I am trying to provide education about the economy and the stock market. To dispel the wrong ideas that have been repeated so long. What is actually happening and why. My second objective is to provide people with an alternative stock trading system that I have developed. A system to trade stocks in this new realistic environment. This system should successfully provide stock market profits and avoid stock market losses. My system functions on both sides of the market, both long and short.

We will get into how my investment is different and how it works later in this book. It is very straightforward and actually quite simple. You can probably run your portfolio with an hour a week and do very well.

The current lack of a knowledge of history is creating problems at this time. To invest properly in the stock market you are going to need to acquire a small amount of knowledge about interest rates. You are going to need to learn about the operation of the Federal Reserve System and its impact on our economy and the stock market.

There is nothing new that is happening today in the stock market or the economy. It has all happened before. This is not the first time that we have encountered high inflation. It is not the first time that the Fed has looked to high interest rates to fight inflation. What is necessary is to look at history and adapt that message to the current situation and market.

The last time the Fed attempted to fight inflation by increasing interest rates was in 1980. Interest rates soared. The effects on inflation were transitory. The stock market went down.

Looking to the future, a knowledge of what has happened in the past will be valuable. It will help to interpret problems as they occur going forward. It is never a simple cut and dried situation. The economy and the stock market and the actions of the Federal Reserve and the actions of the government are always important. History and the resultant market will always tell the story.

Later in this book I will show you how to determine the direction of the market and to determine what your position should be to make a profit and avoid losses. How to position your stock investments,

This book is an attempt to educate you and give you an open mind. We always advocate cutting our losses. We also advocate avoiding extremes. We try to be conservative, yet we recognize that there are risks. The more knowledge that you have of what is going on the better off you are

CHAPTER 4

CONVENTIONAL WISDOM

Virtually all investment advisers adhere to the same general principles. First you are investing for the long-term meaning 5 to 10 years. Second the stock market may go down temporarily but always goes up in the long term. Third your expected average return from owning stocks will be about 6% to 10% per year.

That is the conventional wisdom. The problem is that it does not work any longer. It really never has. For the past 14 years we have had an environment of high liquidity and low interest rates. It has been an expanding economy. That is no longer the situation.

The conventional wisdom does not take into account that our Federal Reserve Bank has clearly stated that they will be increasing interest rates dramatically. They have also stated clearly that they will be reducing liquidity in the money market dramatically. Ignoring information that has been given by the Fed is to ignore reality.

Based upon the Fed's action. It is very apparent that we are headed for a serious recession. This has not happened in the last 14 years. Longer than that. If an investment advisor ignores the information being provided by the Fed he is misleading his clients. The duty of an investment advisor is to keep his clients protected and aware of what is happening in the economy. An investment advisor must anticipate how higher interest rates and reduced liquidity will impact the stock market and their clients investments. This is why the conventional wisdom does not work anymore.

Investment advisers cannot ignore the effect of interest rates and the impact of Fed policy on the securities markets. To do so is ignoring their responsibility as a paid advisor or as a fiduciary. The world is changing. It changed in 2008 when the Fed instituted its policy of high liquidity and low interest rates. The Fed avoided a banking crisis. As I write this book, it is September 2022, we are in the early stage of what I believe will be a serious recession and a prolonged period of high interest rates and reduced liquidity.

The impact of the economic situation will impact the stock market dramatically. The stock market is going down. To ignore this and to look upon it as a temporary and minimal problem is to illustrate a total lack of economics knowledge.

It is the responsibility and duty of an investment advisor of any type to alert his customers and clients of the risks in the stock market. High interest rates and low liquidity cannot be taken lightly or ignored. Protecting the client and avoiding losses is one important part of being an investment advisor. An important part of making a profit in the market is to cut your losses. You must recognize a down market.

The position of the media is not much better. If you listen to the financial news networks the seriousness of increasing interest rates and the reduction of liquidity is not stressed at all. Again the media broadcasters seem to be following the conventional wisdom.

I think the major problem is that brokers,

investment advisers and the people on the media still adhere to the common wisdom. I can understand how that happens. For the past 14 years since 2008 we have had an economy that was very liquid and we had low interest rates. That was the result of the economic crisis of 2007 and 2008. At that time we almost had a very deep recession.

If you recall the Fed had to bail out a number of companies and banks. At that time the Fed did the right thing, the economy turned around and prospered. We avoided a banking crisis.

It is easy to understand how people in the investment management business and stock brokerage firms and the media, have a difficult time saying that we are in a down bear market. That is not good for business. That is also contrary to the message that has been given to clients for years. That does not mean that they should ignore reality.

That was then and this is now. The Fed has started to correct for the excesses of the past. Interest rates are going up and liquidity is going down. The stock market will go down in a weaker economy. The conventional wisdom no longer works. It must be changed for economic reality.

If your investment advisor has told you to be fully invested and to stay the course he has misled you. We are going to have a very deep recession. Interest rates are going to go up substantially. The market is unlikely to recover soon and totally. If you are holding a large portfolio of stocks you should sell them and go to cash. Your stocks will continue to go down in value. If you investment advisor has told you the opposite he is wrong.

Many people have money in an IRA or a 401k and do not really have any advisory services. If you are in that situation you should cut your losses and move your investments into cash equivalents. Whoever administers your plan should be able to tell you how to do that. I talk about these investments later in this book.

It is my philosophy to cut your losses as quickly as you can. You do not have to be fully invested. It is foolish in a down market.

CHAPTER 5

STOCK OWNERSHIP

The ownership of stocks is very broad and stocks are owned by a large portion of the population. In general people own stock through a 401(k) or IRA or some other type of retirement savings plan. Very often these funds are accumulated through employment and unions. For most people stock ownership and stock investment is not their primary interest. It is totally a secondary enterprise. However it usually constitutes a large percentage of a person's total assets.

There are some people, usually in higher income brackets, who accumulate excess assets and invest it in the stock market. These are also people who will have a higher net worth either from an accumulation of funds over time or from other sources such as inheritance and family business.

When you own a share of stock, you own a very tiny piece of a large company. All stock has some value. Generally stocks are traded on the organized stock exchanges in each country. There are approximately 6000 stocks traded on the New York stock exchanges. The number keeps changing there are also stock exchanges in other countries. It is a very large international market.

The price, the value, of a stock goes up and down. It is a free market. Nobody will tell you a reason for the price movement day to day. They may give you their target price. They make comments about the quality of the company and the way it is run. Is is very rare for anybody who is involved in stock investment advice to downgrade a particular stock or industry. In general they will advise to be diversified and to hold on for the long haul, at least five years. The stock market always goes up in the long haul they say..

Everyone gets a statement each month or quarter or so. People look at it. They will remember the overall numbers. As long as it seems to go up over time the public is happy. Secure. The experts are handling their stocks, their money. Big brother is running the stock market. It always goes up, doesn't it?

A lot of people who are invested in this kind of retirement savings account do not have any investment advisory services. They are totally on their own. The plan may have several different ETF's that it can invest in. There is usually a brief description of each fund but no specific investment advice. If you are in this kind of situation, in this market today, you are at a very high risk of losing a substantial amount of your assets. You should move to cash or to a stable fund that does not change in value.

There are many individuals who are well educated and take the time to try and acquire basic knowledge of investing and the economy. However it is rare that they will become very astute. Most people have limited knowledge and depend upon professionals to manage and invest their money.

These professionals are usually part of an investment advisory firm, a stock brokerage firm or a bank. Some are very good. Some are not too good. These people are considered to be experts by the public and may present themselves to the public as experts, In reality most of these individuals have taken the required courses to obtain various federal licenses. They lack any serious knowledge of economics. They have been in the business for a number of years. They talk a good game and are knowledgeable in certain areas but their depth of knowledge is limited.

There are several financial news networks which keep the public informed about the activity in the stock market. The commentators are good-looking intelligent educated people however their education is probably more in the area of media than business and economics. With the exception of one or two who are economists they do not provide more than current statistical information

In general the financial advisors and the television media commentators all fall into the same mold. In general everyone favors the idea of being 100% invested at all times. Holdings of cash is a no-no. Both the investment advisers and the news media promote the idea that the value of stocks always goes up. I can understand how they have come to this conclusion. For the last 14 years we have been in an environment of low interest rates and expanded liquidity. Since the recession of 2008, when the Fed stepped in and eased money and did some bailouts it has been a liquid easy money economy.

One of the things that I do, that most other market participants do not do is to look at history. The economy and the stock market are a two way street, The economy expands and contracts. The stock market goes up and down. To be successful in investing you must be aware of the direction of both interest rates, the economy and the stock market. That is the critical issue and trick. To be in stocks when they go up and short stocks when they go down. You have to go with the flow and recognize that the economy and the market are always subject to change. You must be sensitive to interest rates and changes made by the Fed.

There are no experts. There are individuals who work for companies that have a predetermined agenda. If you are going to make money owning or trading stocks you have to be sufficiently flexible to recognize changes as they occur and to adjust your performance in accordance. It is not a one way market. And it is not a market that will correct for anything given enough time. It is a market where you have to be aware of what is happening and why individual stock issues are going up or going down. Most importantly you must be aware of how the economy and the market have performed going back in history.

If you are stuck in the mold that the market only goes up and in time it will adjust for temporary setbacks you are doomed to failure. You have to figure out if the setback is a decline in an up market or a change to a down bear market. Awareness of the direction of the economy, the market and interest rates are paramount.

Never forget the Fed action in 1979 and 1980. Never forget the recession of July 1981 to November 1982. History is important. Keep in mind the banking crisis of 2008. 1980 lead to higher interest rates and a down market. 2008 led to lower interest rates and expanded liquidity. An upmarket.

It is a two-way Street. The Fed directs the traffic. They will tell you what they are going to do. You have to listen to what they say and act accordingly

CHAPTER 6

THE FED & INTEREST RATES

The Federal Reserve Bank was authorized by Congress in 1913. It is the central bank for the United States. It is run by the Federal Reserve Board. Nickname the Fed.

The Fed has the ability to adjust interest rates and liquidity for the banking system and therefore the economy. They can tighten and loosens money. They can increase or decrease interest rates. They can provide or take away liquidity. If the Fed tightens money we can have a recession or worse. If they loosens money we can have an expansion of the economy. A boom.

The Fed is mandated by Congress to have certain effects on the economy. First the Fed is required to foster full employment and stable prices. Second they must supervise the safety of the banking system. Third they must maintain stability of the financial system. Fourth they must provide services to the federal government and operate the banking payments system.

By controlling interest rates and money liquidity the Fed is controlling the economy. Usually when the economy expands the stock market will go up. Conversely when the economy contracts, recession, the stock market will go down. All major countries have a central bank. Our Federal Reserve Bank is the leader worldwide.

The stock market is a party. It is in reality run by the Fed. They hired the band and own the punch bowl. Everybody is invited. When money is loose, liquidity abundant and interest rates low the Fed will spike the punch bowl. Everybody is happy and the stock market goes up. When money is tight, liquidity stringent and interest rates high, they take away the punch bowl. Everybody is sad and the stock market goes down.

The Fed does not have any secrets. They have 10

meetings per year. They will have an extra meeting if they think it is necessary. They have a press conference after each meeting. They published the minutes of each meeting. They will tell everybody exactly what they are doing. What they expect to do. What they are worried about. They will have extra press meetings to clarify. The Fed wants you to know exactly what it is doing and why they are taking their action. They do not want you to second-guess what they are doing. They want everyone to know what they are doing and why. The Fed has no secrets.

The Fed has announced that they are concerned about the level of inflation. The published statistics for inflation have been in the 7.5% to 8.5% range with a high of 9.1%. The Fed has also announced that the level of liquidity is too high. They have announced that they will be raising interest rates until they see improvement in inflation. They also announced that they will allow their holdings of Treasury and Agency debt to run off and not replace it in the open market. The Fed has told us that they are increasing interest rates and reducing liquidity. In the past the fed has been complacent with a 2% inflation rate.

The Fed has increased the discount rate by 0.25%

in March 2022, by 0.5% in May 2022, by 0.75% in June 2022, by 0.75% in July 2022 and by 0.75% in September 2022. A total of 3% of increases so far in 2022 Increases are expected to continue. The Fed will allow $47.5 billion of bonds monthly to run off through August 2022. It will increase that to $95 billion monthly starting September.

The Fed is increasing interest rates by increasing the Fed funds rate. The Fed is also increasing interest rates by decreasing liquidity in the banking system and not repurchasing federal debt as it matures.. They are putting the burden on the public open market. Reduced liquidity and increased interest rates. A recession is in the works. Stocks go down during a recession.

The last time the Fed conducted an assault on inflation by increasing interest rates was in 1979 and 1980. At the time the Fed pushed their interest rate to 20%. We had a recession in July 1981 to November 1982. A period of 16 months. I cannot find another situation where the Fed has reduced liquidity by allowing federal debt to run off at maturity. I do not think that has happened before. I do expect that it will reduce liquidity dramatically and increase interest rates.

Rule number one: Never fight the Fed. If the Fed is raising interest rates and/or reducing liquidity the strong probability is that we will have a recession. The stock market will go down. Do not own any stocks in this situation. Do not buy the dip. Go to cash. Go to short.

An interest rate inversion is a when short term interest rates are higher than longer term interest rates. The usual situation is for short-term interest rates to be lowest and for interest rates to increase as maturity extends. The official definition of an inversion compares the two-year maturity to the 10 year maturity. In our current situation the interest rate on the two-year and 10 year Treasury crossed, inverted, in early July 2022.

I usually watch the shorter maturities. The one year vs the 10 year. We had an inversion in the yield curve around May of 2022. As I write this book we have a very seriously inverted yield curve. The two-year maturity is at 3.79% and the 10 year yield is at 3.44%. An inversion of 0.35% if we look at the one year it becomes a worse situation.

There is a very strong correlation, almost 100%, between an inversion in the yield curve and a recession. Typically we are looking at a lag of 6 to 18 months between a yield curve inversion and a recession.

Rule number two: Recognize a yield curve inversion. A yield curve inversion tells us that we are likely heading for a recession and that the stock market will go down in anticipation of a recession. As with rule one the stock market is expected to go down Do not own any stock in this situation. Do not buy the dip. Go to cash. Go to short.

The last time that the Fed raised interest rates because of inflation was in 1979 to 1980. At that time the Fed raised its rate to 20%. We subsequently had a recession from July 1981 to November 1982 a period of 16 months.

I do not know or want to project how high interest rates will go in the current situation. However, the prior situation did not have a liquidity problem as we do have now. It is my opinion that the current situation is more difficult. We are starting out at a high level of employment. It seems to me that the employment factor might impact the Fed and reduce its ability to raise interest rates if employment becomes a problem.. At this point that is not a factor.

We should note that's it appears that the Fed was going to embark on this kind of operation at the start of 2000. We did have an interest rate inversion prior to that and the stock market sold off dramatically in early 2000. However the Fed changed its plans when it became apparent that the Covid virus was going to negatively impact the economy very soon. That did happen and we did have a Covid recession. The Stock market had a sharp selloff and then recovered. The interest rate inversion was correct. Covid delayed the Fed plans for two years, but here we are now.

When the Fed increases interest rates it is a very strong indicator that we are going to have a recession and a declining stock market. When we have an interest rate inversion it is a very strong indicator that we are going to have a recession and a declining stock market. The first recent increase by the Fed in interest rates was in March 2022.. The first recent interest rate inversion that we had was also in March 2022.

CHAPTER 7

STOCK MARKET DIRECTION

The idea of trading stocks for profit revolves around the simple concept of being in the right stocks at the right time. The old rule of buy low and sell high or sell high and then buy back low still applies. The question revolves around the direction of the market. Since the market goes both ways there will be times when we want to be long stocks. And there will be times when we want to be short stocks.

My trading system follows the market. I do not have a whole bunch of stock analysts who try to predict earnings and estimate future earnings and multipliers. I think that this is basically a waste of time. I am a market follower and not a market leader. It is my opinion based on my experience that stocks that go in one direction or the other tend to continue in the same direction until something specific happens to change that.

Stock market companies higher armies of analysts to project income and earnings multipliers and then to direct their clients to buy or sell specific stocks. My system is much simpler. I just look at what stocks have been going up or down. Then I buy the best stocks that go up or sell the worst stocks that go down. It is not hard to see which stocks are moving and which are most in style.

Before we pick a stock we have to decide which way the stock market is going. I am writing this book in September 2022. At this time we are in the start of a very strong bear market. So determining market direction is very easy now. But I must presume that a reader will be picking up this book at some time in the future when direction will probably be much less apparent.

The basis of my trading system is to trade with the market. When the market is going up we want to be long stocks when the market is going down we want to be short stocks. When the market is mixed, which happens occasionally, we want to carefully select industries that are going up or down clearly. If we are confused and don't have a firm conviction, the sidelines are the best choice. I am a strong believer in cut your losses. The market will decide on direction in time.

There are a number of factors that come into play in determining the direction of the stock market. The most important is actions by the Fed as well as interest rates. As a hard and fast rule when interest rates are being dramatically increased by the Fed the stock market is going to take a downward direction. By dramatically increased I mean more than a one quarter of a point increase. I mean consistent increases and other factors.

In the last chapter we discussed the actions of the Fed. We also talked about interest rate inversion. Those two factors are still the most important in determining the future market director. However at some time in the future things will be less clear.

Although the action of the Fed and interest rate inversion remain primary I have other indicators that I use. There are three other factors that I use to determine the direction of the stock market.

First is earnings per share. This is a concept that was put forward by authors Ben Graham and David Dodd in their book Security Analysis, first published in 1934. Stocks of companies that earn money are worth more than stocks of companies that do not. Growing earnings are more valuable than stagnant earnings and deserve a higher price. This is basic security analysis. If stocks earn money they should go up in value.

The second parameter that influences stock value is style or fad. Dress styles change. Stocks go in and out of style also. They captivate analysts and become a fad. When one stock analyst likes a particular company others tend to follow. The more that follow the more that a stock is in style, a fad. The higher the price the higher the earnings multiplier. Over the years there have been different market styles that pushed stocks in one direction or another. For example at one time Internet stocks were in style a fad. Many stocks went up without any earnings just because of the business that they were in. Or some wild and whimsical projected plans. Style will influence the value of a stock or a group of stocks.

The next factor that we use to look at stock market direction is the popular averages. I follow the S&P 500 average, the NASDAQ average and the Russell 2000. As a general rule the direction of a moving average will indicate the direction of the market. For example in up trending markets the average will the above its 200 day moving average almost all of the time. In a down trending market the price will be below its 200 day moving average. We also looked at the 50 day moving average.

We look at the general configuration of the major averages. If you look at a graph of the averages and superimpose the 200 day moving average you will see that all of the indexes crossed their moving average in March 2022. The NASDAQ has never come back above its 200 day moving average to date. The S&P 500 and the Russell 2000 have come back over their 200 day moving average briefly.

If you look at the shape of the one year graphs of the averages all three are configured into a rounding top. Charts of the averages over the past year or two are decidedly negative.

In summary we had the first increase in interest rates by the Fed in March 2022. We had an inversion of the one year and 10 year Treasury interest rates in March 2022. We had all three major averages go below their 200 day moving average in March 2022. Very convincing evidence of a bear. March 2022 is a good pick for the start date.

The market direction indicators that I discuss in this chapter are for the most part judgmental. Except for an interest rate inversion, which is specific, and the Fed taking a definitive action, also specific. The other indicators require examination and judgment.

Most of the time we cannot depend upon interest rate inversion or action by the Fed. They do not happen constantly. We don't want to have the necessity of making a judgmental decision on the direction of the market if we can avoid it.

Our trading and investment methodology revolves around trading and investing in the market with recognition of the direction of the various sectors. As I said it is our objective to be long stocks that are going up in value. It is also our objective to be short stocks that are going down in value. At any time and in any situation where there is a question as to the direction of the market we cut our losses and go to the sidelines. It is better to be out of the market than to make a mistake and take a loss.

My Market Segment Direction Analysis tool is designed to help determine direction. I have developed this tool to have a more clear picture of stock market direction. It is not perfect and does require a little bit of judgment but it is a tool that is fairly effective most of the time. After you have used it for a short time you will be able to judge market direction fairly well. I fully describe this tool in the next chapter. It has nothing to do with conventional wisdom.

CHAPTER 8

WEINTRAUB'S MARKET SEGMENT DIRECTION ANALISYS

Market Segment Analysis is the most important parameter that I look at. It tells us exactly what is moving in the market. What is going up and what is going down. Looking at this does require a little bit of judgment at times but it is not very complex. What we are really looking at is the relative movement of market sectors in comparison to the movement of indexes and over time.

The S&P 500 is considered to be made up of 11 market segments. They are called the GICS,

Global Industry Classification Standards. Since the start of the ETF, Exchange Traded Funds, industry around 1990 the industry has grown enormously. There are now 2952 ETF's on the US markets and it is growing. ETF's are developed and issued to the public by a host of issuing companies. There are ETF's that mimic every industry imaginable, every index, every sub industry and every style of trading. There are some that are small and some that are very large. They are publicly traded and made up of the individual stocks that we trade.

If you are going to invest in and trade stocks, you are going to need an account with a stock brokerage company. All of these companies have available to their clients one or more software programs. These programs are available for trading but they also are available for stock analysis. They are usually free. I have found that these programs are quite good and are very similar from one company to the other.

I personally use a program provided by Charles Schwab, This is my personal choice. You can choose any programs provided by any broker you wish. They are all very similar and mostly free.

You are going to need a program that allows you

to construct several watch lists A watch list is a list of individual stocks or ETF's. You can track them and do various comparisons using the software. You will want to be able to track the performance of an ETF in comparison to a benchmark like the S&P 500 index. You also want to be able to track the year to date or some other fixed time period for performance.

You will probably also need a screener program. The stockbroker that you use should also give you a program that can give a full description of various stocks and other items like publicly traded ETF descriptions.

This may sound complicated but it really is not. The software programs are well developed and easy to use. You can usually call your broker and ask for help. Your stockbroker will be very accommodating. You are their client.

There are a large number of ETF's for the 11 GICS sectors. Every fund family seems to have one. There is little difference between them. Below is my typical list that I have used. Copy it. This is your first watch list Call it GICS sectors.

ETF	SECTOR

XLB	MATERIALES
XLI	INDUSTRIALS
XLF	FINANCIALS
XLE	ENERGY
XLY	CONSUMER DISCRETIONARY
XLK	TECHNOLOGY
XLC	COMMUNICATIONS
XLV	HEALTH
XLP	CONSUMER DURABLES
XLU	UTILITYS
VNQ	REAL ESTATE

If you look at the GICS watch list today, mid September 2022, in your software, and compare ETFs to the S & P 500 Index you will see the sectors that are out performing the S & P 500 index up and down. You can also do a comparison for Year to Date movement. Again you will see those sectors that are up and down. You can click at the top of each list and arrange the sector ETFs in ascending or descending order. A very simple way to see the action of the market by each sector. No experts required. No mystery.

Of the 11 sectors almost all are down, one is neutral and one is up. That is 82% are negative. Obviously a down market. We cannot expect that this analysis will always be tilted strongly in one direction as it is now. In general it is going to be more like a 60/40 split. Or a 70/30 split. That would still indicate a down or up market.

When you look at the GICS watch list for the markets sectors you want to arrange them in an ascending or descending order. Then it will be very apparent what segments are going up in price or going down in price. You can do this comparison against the S&P 500 index or a fixed period of time such as a year to date. You will easily see the market direction. It is that simple. The watch list scan will tell us exactly which segments of the market are going up or down. It will indicate the proportion and direction. It will indicate strongly up or strongly down. Or mixed or neutral.

As I write this book my indicator is decidedly negative. That did not happen all at once. Sectors began to show up as trending down in December 2021. When that first happens it means that you get out of those sectors that are negative. As time went on more sectors showed up as negative. January, February, March.

By April my market segment direction tool clearly indicated that the market had turned negative. That coincided with the first interest raise by the Fed and the first interest rate inversion. By that time if you are following my system you should have been out of the market, long. You should have been accumulating short positions. That is how you avoid taking major losses. You get out of the week segments first. Then you can begin to accumulate short positions in weak segments as the market weakens.

In the next chapter we will talk about how to pick companies that are moving with their segments of the market. That is the critical selection. The idea is to buy stocks that are going up and to sell short stocks that are going down.

I invented this tool for determining stock market direction. It works because it does not require any computations or mysterious mumbo jumbo. It just looks at what is happening in the market.

As is said in the above chapter 7, I also look at a watch list that contains the major indexes. These are the S&P 500, SPY, the NASDAQ, QQQ and the Russell 2000, IWM. These are the ETFs for the indexes. These indexes are looked at mostly for confirmation.

You can also look at any of these sector ETF's and index ETF's in your scanner. You should be able to see how each sector and index is performing in relationship to a 200 day and 50 day simple moving average. Also you can look at any of the popular technical indicators. Primarily for your education. Using them for stock selection and market direction is quite a chore and I find not necessary and useless.

Rule number three: Only buy stocks that are in industries that are going up. Always sell short stocks that are in industries that are going down. Always cut your losses

I am going to talk about short selling. There are some people who have a negative attitude about short selling. They say things that make little sense concerning morals and selling something that you do not own. In reality there is nothing wrong or different or high risk about short selling. It is the safest way to make a profit in a down market. We are not advocating the use of margin or getting over extended. All we are doing is to sell a stock today and buy it back a month or two from now at a lower price for profit.

If you are really vehemently against short selling you can always look at one of the negative ETF's. They do the same thing but more broadly.

CHAPTER 9

STOCK SELECTION

We have now determined the direction of the stock market. Our next job is to decide what to buy or sell. As I have said before I am writing this book in September 2022. We are in a bear market so I will illustrate stock selection for a bear market. At some time in the future we will be in a bull market. Stock selection is the same except you will choose up instead of down industries and stocks.

To analyze the market for primary market direction we used the GICS 11 market segments. When it comes to stock selection we are going to get more detailed and use a list of 30 industry ETF's. What this lists really amounts to is the 11 GICS segments divided into more individual industries and added. I think that this better reflects the economy and the market. This is going to be your third watch list we will call it INDUSTRIES WATCHLIST.

The first was GICS market segments. The second was the MAJOR STOCK INDEX list. The third watch list we will call simply INDUSTRIES. There are a very large number of ETF's mimicking individual industries. This list is my source. With experience you may want to add or delete a particular ETF. That is entirely your option. The system will work the same. It is very basic and strait forward.

Below is my Industry Watch list. You can copy it into a watch list for your own use in your software. There are 30 ETFs. When you are more experienced with the system you can make additions or deletions.

ETF	INDUSTRY
XRT	RETAIL
XPH	PHARMA
XOP	OIL & GAS EXP

XME	METALS & MINING
XLY	CONSUMER STAP
XLV	HEALTH
XLU	UTILITIES
XLP	CONSUMER DISC
XLK	TECHNOLOGY
XLI	INDUSTRIAL
XLG	TOP 50
XLF	FINANCIAL
XLE	ENERGY
XLC	COMUNICATIONS
XLB	MATTERIALS
XHS	HEALTH CARE SVCS
XHE	HEALTH CARE EQPT
XHB	HOME BUILDERS
XES	OIL & GAS EQUIP
XAR	AEROSPACE
VNQ	REAL ESTATE
SMH	SEMICONDUCTORS
OIH	OIL SERVICES
KRE	REGIONAL BANKS
KIE	INSURANCE
KBWY	REIT
JETS	AIRLINES
IYE	ENERGY
IBB	BIOTECHNOLOGY
GDX	GOLD MINERS

You will load this Industry ETF watch list into

your computer software. The software should be able to produce a screen that will give you the price performance of the individual ETF's against a fixed time period. Up or down. It is also useful to run a comparison against the S & P 500.

By clicking on the top of the row called Price Change YTD, year to date, the individual ETF's will line up in order. The largest decline will be at the top and the smallest decline at the bottom. You can click again and the order will reverse. Simply put you can see what industries in the market have going up and down for the year to date. You can also do a comparative performance vs. the S&P 500. The results should be the same.

We previously looked at the GICS watch list to determine the direction of the market as a whole. We now have broken the market into industries and have arrange them so that we can see which industries are the worst performers and which are the best performers.

As a general observation of market performance stocks tend to continue moving in the same direction until there is a major change in the market. For example stocks that go up over time continue to go up over time. Stocks that go down tend to continue to go down over time. If the market is in a bear market it is of course subject to bear market rallies. In a bull market it is subject to bull market selloffs.

You may have heard the reference to a stock as being overboard or oversold. I do not think that there is such a thing. Stocks continue to move in the same direction. Overbought or oversold probably refers to the speed of increase or decrease in price.

I have given you a list of 30 industries. It is by no means complete. You are free to add additional industries to the list. It is really a question of how much time you want to spend looking at the individual industries to pick your stocks.

By looking at the watch list for the industries we can see easily the direction that each industry is moving in. We already have determined the primary market direction. If it is up we want to look at industries that are up and if it is down we want to look at industries that are down.

Now we have determined which industries are most likely to have stocks that we are interested in. In the next chapter we will discuss how to set up your portfolio. The point is that you cannot look at all of the perhaps 6000 stocks listed on the various exchanges. That is probably not worth the time and effort to add another issue to our universe. We have to draw the line someplace. What we're doing is relying on the expertise of the analyst who runs the particular ETF. You want to have a reasonable amount of diversification. That does not mean mixing market directions. It means mixing industries.

We should take note that our universe is 30 ETF's. We can assume that each one will have 15 to 20 stocks. Simple arithmetic says that we are dealing with a universe of perhaps 500 to 600 stocks depending on duplication. We should note that each of the ETF's is run by a securities analyst. That person is picking what he thinks are the best stocks in the industry. We are assuming that he has picked the representative stocks for that industry. There may be other companies and it is entirely your discretion to decide if you want to look at other stocks in the same industry.

However we have to recognize that whoever is running the particular ETF is probably meeting other analysts and managers at industry gatherings. I am sure that particular stocks are very much the subject discussion. As I said earlier in this book one of the factors that determines a stock's price is its style or fad.

Generally speaking I think the stock issues in the individual ETF's are probably the most popular stocks in their industry.

As I have said earlier it is totally in your discretion to add or delete an industry from the watch list You can also expand the watch list to include a larger number of industries represented by ETF's. However you have to keep in mind that if you do that you are going to wind up spending more time looking at the ETF's and the individual stocks. It is a question whether it is worth the additional time compared to different results.

The basic thing to keep in mind is that you want to only by stocks in industries that are going up. You only want to sell short stocks in industries that are going down. It is unusual for one particular stock to go against the trend of its industry. It can happen I guess, but is it worth the risk. Do not fall in love with a particular stock.

CHAPTER 10

HOW TO PICK STOCKS

We have determined the direction of the market. We have divided the market into industries and we have arrange the industries in order of their performance. The next task is to decide which stocks we are going to put into our portfolio. As I have said before I am writing this book in September 2022. We are presently in a bear market so I am going to do selections for a bear market as illustration for you. At some time in the future we will be in a bull market I expect. The procedure is exactly the same but reversed for market direction.

Since we know the direction of the various industries we can simply look at the individual stocks that are owned by those particular ETF's. By clicking on the SYMBOL for the individual ETF in your watch list, your software should take you to the page for that particular ETF. Today the worst performing ETF on our industry list is XLK down 41.96 YTD. Technology.

When you get to the page for the individual ETF the stocks that are owned by that ETF are arranger by percentage of net assets in the left hand column. There is a second column to the right labeled YTD %. (Year to Date %). Numbers in red are declining stocks, Numbers in black are advancing stocks. You can click at the top of the column and rearrange in ascending or descending order. You should be able to scroll down and look at the individual stocks that the ETF owns.

The top stock on the right-hand column at this time is Cisco Systems. Down 35.96% for the year so far. That is our first pick for a stock to short. If we click on the symbol for the stock we are taken to the page for the stock. We can then look at the chart of the stock and superimpose on it the moving averages. Having done that we can see that the stock remains well below its 200 day moving average. The market price for the stock is 40.50. More than ample room for the stock to continue moving down.

The second stock from the top of the right hand column is Uber Technologies. Down 35.87% year to date. That is our second candidate for a short sale. When we click on the symbol for the stock it takes us to the page for the stock. We can now look at the chart and superimpose the moving averages on it. Although the stock had a bear market rally recently it is below its 200 day moving average. At today's price of $27.57 it is a little on the low side for a short sale, but still enough space to decline. This is our second short sale choice.

Looking at the right hand column again, the third stock down from the top is Broadcom down 30.53% for the year. Again the procedure is the same. Again the stock is below its 200 day moving average. This time the market price is $464.75. That means you might sell short an odd lot. It should not create a problem.

And so we continue on with the fourth stock from the top. The procedure is exactly the same. Now we have four stocks from the technology ETF.

We want to have diversification of 20 individual stock issues. Simple arithmetic. We will take the five best or worst performing ETF's, depending upon our determination of market direction. We will then pick the best or worst performing stocks from each ETF.

Now we go to the second down ETF in our industry list. That is the Semi Conductor industry. We do exactly the same procedure and pick four stocks from that industry

If we pick five ETF's and then take the four best or worst stocks from each of the ETF's we will have 20 stock issues. Write them down in a list. There is of course the possibility of duplication. That is the same stock may be owned by two different ETF's. We simply eliminate the duplication and pick another stock.

Our method of picking stocks is really very simple. We do not have analysts making projections of earnings and performance. Those projections are really useless to us. We are looking at only the directional movement of individual stocks. We are assuming that the stocks will continue to move in the same direction. When we look at history, that is what has happened.

We can do a little bit of analysis on our own part. We can put our portfolio of stocks into a watch list We can check the performance of each stock by its moving averages. You should be able to get that information on the individual page for each stock. If we are in a bear market the stocks in our portfolio should always be below their 200 day moving average. They should also usually be below their 50 day moving average. In a bull market the opposite. If a stock moves against us in direction we simply sell and move on to another stock.

Rule Number Four. Cut your losses. Never hold a stock that is moving against you for too long on the hopes that it will turn. This is the recipe for disaster and big losses.

Once you get this system started, you should be able to do all of the work in about an hour once a week. The first time should take you longer.

Do not obsess about your stock investments and trading. Do not over supervise what you are doing. Relax. It is very rare that the market will move dramatically and by surprise. If it is going to move dramatically you will know it before hand because there will be an obvious signal.

You must stay aware of actions by the Fed. You must stay aware of an inversion of interest rates. Follow your trades but do not get over involved.

Keep in mind that the relative position of the stocks in your industry watch list will change from week to week. The industry position will change week to week. The stock positions will change from week to week.

Once you make a commitment to a particular stock your objective is to hold it until there is a reason to sell. That reason will be the stock price moving through the 200 day moving average and the 50 day moving average. Also you want to see that the industry has not had a direction change.

The other thing that you must be concerned with is a large rally in a bear market or a large selloff in a bull market. Sometimes these events can be startling. Before you panic take a look at the major indexes with the moving averages superimpose. If the major averages have not penetrated their 200 day moving average wait to see what happens. It's the market is still subject to an interest rate inversion or the Fed can be expected to continue their monetary policy wait

wait before you do anything. Do not be fooled by a bear market rally or a bull market selloff. Don't get tired holding a stock. Some stocks moves slowly and some move rapidly. Some markets are slow and some markets are fast. Always look at the major market averages with their moving averages superimpose. Always look at your stocks with the moving averages also superimpose. Don't get fooled by short-term surprising market moves. There are a lot of unsophisticated investors who may jump into a market before they are properly informed.

In the next chapter I will discuss how to put together a portfolio of stocks. Done diversification is extremely important to protect you from taking a major loss.

CHAPTER 11

SETTING UP YOUR PORTFOLIO

I stated earlier in this book that we wanted to have diversification. The main reason for diversification is basically to spread our risk. I have mentioned several times before that I believe very strongly in cutting our losses. By having diversification effectively one stock issue cannot hurt you if you are wrong.

As an investor and as a stock trader you want to have diversification. I typically suggest that a portfolio should have 20 stocks at any particular time. Doing the simple arithmetic, if you have

$100,000 to invest, then each of your stock commitments should be $5000. 5% of your total portfolio. From the standpoint of diversification you would like to have 20 stocks. Also from the standpoint of diversification those stocks should be spread over five industries. That is four stocks for each industry. That is 20 stock issues, five industries and four stocks per industry.

For example if a particular stock commitment is 5% of your portfolio and you lose 20% of the value of that stock, your net loss is only 1% of your total portfolio. That is not a major problem.

It is the structure and diversification of your portfolio that gives you protection. What I have outlined above gives a maximum commitment of 5% of your portfolio to any individual stock. Therefore if you are wrong on a particular stock you will not have a devastating loss.

Many investors make the basic mistake of having too high a concentration in one particular stock. Yes in theory if you're right the stock will go up and you will make a bundle. However if you are wrong the opposite will happen and you will have a large loss. I don't think I'm that smart. To pick the one that best stock in the world that is going to go up dramatically. I do not think it is worth the risk to have a large concentration in one stock compared to the more secure situation of limiting your individual positions. It is your bet. Yes it is a bet, not a trade or investment.

Initially when you first start using this system you may already own some stocks. Your first task in implementing this system is to determine the direction of the stock market. As I have said I have illustrated in the prior chapter exactly how to pick stocks to buy or to sell short in this market. So that is your first task to get rid of your positions that are on the wrong side of the market before further deterioration and loss. Your second task is to run our program and determine a group of stocks to put into your portfolio. Previously stated, I wrote this book in September 2022. We are now in a bear market. The Fed has already raised interest rates and they will continue to raise interest rates. The Fed is also going to allow part of its bond portfolio to run off. This puts more upward pressure on interest rates. It is my opinion that we are presently in the early stages of a substantial recession. I also think that we are going to see considerably higher interest rates. The result is going to be a continuation of the decline of the stock market.

Having said that if you are coming to this system and presently own stocks, you may be on the wrong side of this market. Let's not play around we are in a bear market. If you own stocks the chances are that you are going to lose part of your investment. Therefore your first move is to immediately place a sell order and clear the decks. Cut your losses.

There is the possibility that you presently have some stocks that are short positions. If that is the case your first task is to look at the charts of each stock to determine its relationship to its moving averages. All short stock positions should pass the criteria of our method of selection. As I have said we believe in cutting our losses. That means we do not want to own any stocks unless they are performing properly with the market. Check the Industries that your stocks are in. You have to use your judgment. If their industry is performing badly then you can keep old short positions,

As time goes on you should monitor your portfolio if the stocks that you have committed to are no longer among the stocks in the top five or bottom five industry groups you should examine them carefully if they move above or below their moving average, then you should consider eliminating the position.

Basically you want to have most of your commitment, short or long in the five worst or best performing industries. If you find that a stock that you own is no longer performing as you expected you can dispose of it and get another stock in another industry.

I do not recommend that investors use a margin accounts purchase stock. A margin account is borrowing money. That is not investment, it is speculation.

Always remember that there is nothing wrong with being out of the market at a particular time. Being out of the market, in cash, is a safe position. Your object is to make a profit with reasonably low risk. You do not want to be married to a stock. Keep your portfolio fresh.

CHAPTER 12

WHEN TO CHANGE DIRECTION

We have discussed market direction and investing in stocks. All good things come to an end. At some point we are going to have to change our portfolio. This will be primarily because of a change in the market direction.

We are market followers not market leaders. You must remain aware of changes in Fed policy and any interest rates inversion. These do not happened that frequently. You should run the GICS watch list on a regular basis. This will probably be your first indication that market direction is changing. Expect the indicator to move to mixed before it moves dramatically in one direction or the other.

If there is a change in direction of the GICS watch list your first move should be to the sidelines, cash. If the GICS is changing it could take a month or so to really show a new direction or there could be a sharp change. The conservative answer remains moving to cash until direction is established. Until you feel confident. Don't get fooled.

If the market moves from negative, its current position, to positive it will probably show a split direction before things become firm. I do not think that we will see that kind of move until the Fed changes its tight money policy.

Generally bear markets are shorter in duration and steeper and quicker. Bull markets are slower more steady and considerably longer. When stocks enters a bear market we can have a dramatic decline. Sometimes a market bottom can be sharp. In a longer bear market the bottom is slower and more rounding. A bull market can be a slow rounding top. In general a bear market can be sharp so we could miss the initial thrust. However I think that the present bear market has a way to go, I think that it will end with a whimper and not a boom. I think that we will see the bottom coming. There should be a change in Fed policy before a bottom. As I have said before the Fed does not keep secerits. They will tell you before they change policy.

I am writing this book in September 2022. We are presently in a bear market. I cannot guess exactly when and where it is going to end. There are too many variables. We started from extremely low interest rates and from an enormous amount of federal debt held on the balance sheet of the Fed. To compound the problem we also started with a low unemployment rate. It is my opinion that the one thing that could stop the Fed is a large increase in the unemployment rate. That is a totally unknown factor. Unemployment could increase slowly or it could go up quickly. I have no idea and I don't think anyone else does either.

If you suspect a direction change for the market you must expect that the Fed has stopped increasing interest rates and has stopped allowing its portfolio to run off. If the fed is still raising interest rates the chances are that the bear market will continue.

The experts who practice the conventional wisdom look for a sharp V bottom when the market changes direction. That happens from time to time. However you cannot look upon every bear market rally as a bottom. That is foolishness and can lead to buying stocks far too early, before a real bottom. That can lead to large losses.

We are going to have to play this by ear. I am not going to guess what is going to happen. toss a coin and say 50%?

It is worthwhile to look at recessions and bear markets that have happened in the past markets. Most bear markets last between one and two years. I do not think that the current bear market is any different, unknown duration. At some time in the future the market will turn around. Your guess is as good as mine. I do think that we will see it coming. If you are unsure cash is always safe.

When we do get a turnaround in direction, we should first see the Fed stop doing negative money tightening things or at least let us know that there is a change coming. As I have said previously, the Fed does not keep secrets. They will tell you when they are going to change their stance.

It may be worthwhile to look at past markets In general bull markets are much longer than bear markets. Bull markets can last as long as 10 years or more. Bear markets run between one and two years. Typically bull markets have a more rounding and segmented top. You can see this by doing your market segment analysis. Segments will start to change and it will usually take some time for you see a strong change in market direction. Bear markets can have either a sharp V bottom or a more rounding bottom.

We had a bear market from January 1972 to September 1974. The market declined 48%. The bottom was two lows about a month apart. I will call that a rounding bottom. We had a recession from December 1976 to February 1978. The market declined 20% with a slow rounding bottom.

We had a recession from November 1980 through August 1982. That was the last time that the Fed attacked inflation by raising interest rates. Interest rates went as high as 20%. The market decline was 28%.

We had a recession that started November 2000 and ended in August 2002. The market declined 48%. There was a rounding bottom. We had a recession that started in November 2007. It ended in March 2009. The decline was 56%. That was the start of the low interest rate and high liquidity era. That market had a rounding bottom. That was the banking crises of 2008.

We had a brief recession from February 2000 thru March 2000. That was a very short but steep recession. The Covid recession. The market lost 56% of its value. There was a sharp V shape to bottom.

Here we are today our market made a rounding top with a market high on the S&P 500 of 4798. Your guess of the bottom and my guess are just as good. Do you want to guess at a 50% decline? In good time we will know.

CHAPTER 13

MANAGING YOUR 401k

There are a lot of people who own a 401(k) or IRA through the company for which they work or through a union. In general these savings / retirement plans are administered by one of the large stock brokerage companies or investment management firms or Investment Banks. Almost universally these plans are set up based on the conventional wisdom. Stocks always go up, if they go down it is a minor setback, time will fix everything. The conventional wisdom does not work.

If you own one of these plans at present and have not taken any action the chances are that you have substantial losses. Typically these plans can be invested in a limited number of ETF's. By limited number I mean not more than a dozen. The chances are that at this point you have a substantial loss in your account. Most of these accounts do not have an ETF that you can buy that is stable and avoid going down if the market goes down. Most do not have available a negative ETF that will go up when the market goes down. If there is nothing else that you can do you should have your plan put your money into a money market fund. The people who run these accounts are fiduciary s. However in general they do not seem to be bothered by the market and their employees taking a loss..

My advice to you is that if you are in a bear market without the possibility of investing in other than a few ETF's that you should move your entire investment into a money market and sit on the sidelines. I would also suggest that you complain to the human resources department of your company about the shortcomings of the plan that they have provided for their employees.

Next time a self-directed 401k is far superior if that can be accomplished in the plan.

An IRA or 401(k) with and an investment advisor

that you have personally contracted with should have an arrangement where you can shelter yourself from a bear market. If your investment advisor will not accommodate your needs, get a different investment advisor who will accommodate you.

If you're plan can be self administered then you can handle its investments like any other portfolio. Being in a 401(k) or IRA is primarily a tax delay mechanism. It should not prevent you from acting properly in a bear market. The idea of a plan is to accumulate money for later retirement. Limiting investments does not do that.

CHAPTER 14

THE RECASSION OF JULY 1981 TO NOV. 1982

The last time that the Fed undertook to control inflation by raising interest rates was in 1979 and 1980. At that time the federal funds rate went as high as 20%. We had a recession resulting from the Fed interest rate increases. The recession was from July 1981 through November 1982 a period of 16 months. Unemployment got 11%. Slow economic activity continued well into the next two years. This was the worst recession since the great depression of the 1930s

If you compare our situation today with the inflation of 1980 there are two important differences. First we have the problem of a huge amount of federal debt that is owned by the Federal Reserve. We have not seen this situation in the past. Yet we are trying to reduce the balance sheet amount. In addition we have a very high rate of employment at this time.

The Fed will continue its policy of increased interest rates and reduction in the amount of federal debt owned until they run into a problem. In 1982 the problem was a recession and high unemployment. But we did not start off with a positive employment situation and very low interest rates at that time. In addition there was not a debt portfolio to liquidate.

There is a relationship between interest rates and unemployment. It is illustrated by what is called the Phillips curve. As interest rates increase unemployment increases and inflation decreases. So there is a relationship. The question comes down to how much we can raise interest rates while restringing the economy. The problem is that we can't let unemployment get out of hand. In other words when we raise interest rates we are going to create a recession. How bad a recession can we have in the name of reduced inflation. How much unemployment can we take. We started with low unemployment at this time.

The Fed has raised interest rates by 3% total to now. Unemployment remains low. The big question is how high interest must go before unemployment goes up.

Add to the situation the fact that we are also trying to reduce the amount of federal debt owned by the Fed. The net effect of putting the burden of replacing federal debt on the public market is effectively increasing interest rates further. It is a very complex situation that we have not had in the past.

Further complicating the situation is that as we raise interest rates the US dollar becomes more attractive to foreigners. Basically as we raise interest rates our currency goes up in value. Foreign currencies go down in value. Foreign goods become cheaper for us to buy. On the other hand foreigners are getting less dollars for their products. Essentially we are exporting our inflation.

There are all kinds of problems associated with increasing interest rates and allowing debt to run off. What will probably halt the increase in interest rates sometime in the future is either the Fed has produced too much recession or they have created impossible problems for other countries. At some point in the future the Fed will stop there monetary policies. We have no idea when and at what interest rate level that will happen. It is not a simple answer that is going to be over quickly

In the past the Fed has not been successful at reducing inflation other than temporarily by increasing interest rates.

Until the Fed changes its policy of increasing interest rates to reduce inflation we can expect to see interest rates continue to climb. At this time we have not seen any measurable change in inflation and the unemployment rate. I would expect that the present policy of the Fed will continue for quite some time.

I do not expect to see interest rates go as high as they did in 1980, 20%. I do think that we are still quite a way from a change in Fed policy. That means that we can expect to see a continuation of the bear market.

Until the Fed sets its sites to discontinue the policy of higher interest rates to reduce inflation we can not expect to see a change in the market. We should not be looking for a sharp reversal.

Once the Fed decides to change policy they will be very gradual in reducing interest rates. Unfortunately there is an no way that we can predict when the progression of increased interest rates will end. Suffice it to say that we know at some point it will end. We do not know where.

What I am suggesting is that the change in market direction will not be immediately dramatic. That is why the GICS watch list indicator is valuable. As the market changes direction different segments of the market will begin to show direction changes in the watch list

CHAPTER 15

WHERE DID THE INFLATION COME FROM

Why do we have inflation in the 7.5% to 8.5% range? What causes inflation. It seems like it has been with us forever. This is not the first time that the Fed has become concerned with inflation.

Basically inflation comes from two sources. It can be the result of expanded monetary liquidity. It can also be the result of an imbalance between supply and demand for goods. Since inflation can come from supply demand imbalance it can be controlled theoretically by reducing demand. A recession reduces demand because in a recession unemployment increases. If interest rates go up a recession is more likely. Therefore increasing interest rates theoretically should reduce inflation.

The other source of inflation is an expanded money supply, expanded liquidity. That is a nice way of saying that we have been printing money. The major reason for inflation is printing money, easy credit. The Fed controls the money supply. By that I mean that they can expand the money supply.

If you look at the money in your pocket you will see that you are actually carrying around Federal Reserve Notes. They are denominated in dollars but they are issued by the Federal Reserve Bank. The US central bank. Money is not issued by the Treasury Department.

Now let's say that the US government wants to buy $1 billion of missiles. They go to the missile manufacturer and say we want $1 billion of missiles. The missile manufacturer gives them $1 billion of missiles and says pay me. The government goes to the Federal Reserve Bank and says here is our Treasury note for $1 billion. The Fed takes the treasury note and deposits $1 billion to the government's account. The government then pays the missile company. We have just created $1 billion of money.

It does not have to work that way. Instead of giving the Treasury note to the Federal Reserve Bank the government can sell a Treasury note in the open market. That uses money that is already in existence. No new money is created. The problem is that if the Treasury sells a note in the open market it puts pressure on the money supply and causes interest rates to go up. If the Fed buys the Treasury note and puts it on its balance sheet it does not put upward pressure on interest rates. Putting a Treasury note on the balance sheet of the Fed as opposed to selling it in the public market is a deliberate decision that increases the money supply, liquidity.

In 2008 we had a financial crisis in the US. You may remember it as a time when the Federal Reserve had to bail out various banks and other financial institutions. You may also remember it as the time when Lehman Brothers went bankrupt. At the time it was the fourth largest investment banking company in the US. At the time the Fed also provided bail out financing for a number of other financial institutions.

The financial crisis of 2008 produce a pretty stiff

recession. Unemployment started to go up. Interest rates started to go up. We were about to have a very difficult economy. It all revolved around the sale of low quality mortgages. A number of banks and financial institutions were in distress.

The Fed stepped in. They reduced interest rates and they increase liquidity in the banking system dramatically. The method they use for increasing liquidity was to buy federal debt and agency debt directly. The financial crisis of 2008 was averted. The Fed continue their policy of low interest rates and high liquidity for a number of years. The economy did well. Unemployment declined. A lot of the liquidity found its way into the stock market and then housing.

The Fed balance sheet contains approximately $9 trillion of Treasury securities and mortgage backed securities. The Fed program is to allow to run off $47.5 billion of securities monthly through August 2022. Subsequently it will be increased to $95 billion monthly. It is going to take quite a number of years to allow all of these securities to run off.

Allowing securities to run off and requiring the open market to replace the money puts a heavy upward pressure on interest rates. This program of reducing the balance sheet of the Fed will in itself put tremendous upward pressure on interest rates for a considerable period of time.

The Fed originally tried to start this program around the year 2000. Everything was set to go and then the Covid pandemic showed up. Instead of being able to raise interest rates and liquidate balance sheet holdings, the Fed found that it had to reverse course. Money remained easy and instead of allowing bonds to run off the Fed had to continue purchasing bonds to bolster the economy during the pandemic. The current program was delayed because of the pandemic. Barring any unforeseen situation it appears that it is going to go ahead full steam now.

We are probably going to be living with higher interest rates for some time to come.

You could question whether the Fed did the right thing. They loosened money and expanded liquidity. They prevented a banking system and an economic collapse. They made the temporary bargain of accepting increased inflation in exchange for a functioning economy. When you get right down to it. The primary interest of the Fed is to maintain and hopefully expand the US economy. I think the Fed did the right thing.

So here we are. The Fed is trying to reverse its policies of the last 10 or more years. We have never been in this exact situation before. Economic literature is clear. When interest rates go up, unemployment goes up and demand goes down and inflation goes down. In economics that is cold the Phillips curve.

The question is how is reducing liquidity by allowing debt to run off going to succeed. In the interim interest rates are going up. We are going to have a recession. We have to watch how this all plays out. How is r running off debt going to affect demand and inflation. The hope is that inflation will go down.

Quite frankly, I do not think that anyone has a definitive answer for the this question. We will see what happens in the next few months.

CHAPTER 16

INTEREST RATES, P/E RATIOS AND CAP RATES

There is a relationship between interest rates and price earnings multipliers and capitalization rates. From the standpoint and of an individual investor the interest rate received from a bank deposit is a no risk return on capital. That is because principal deposited in a interest-bearing bank account is guaranteed by the FDIC. There is no risk to principle and a set interest rate return on capital. There are other risk less investments that return income on capital. For example there are Treasury securities.

As we go up the curve and add a little bit of risk,

to the rates of return offered theoretically the rate of return should increase. Our movements into a higher interest rate environment is still new. It is easy to assume that given a few months we will soon see competitive deposit rates from financial institutions. These companies are simply middleman. We should soon see a spectrum of returns and maturities. I think it is a safe assumption to think that we will soon see returns that were offered by these institutions 10 or more years ago.

When we look at a stock we are looking at an investment that has some degree of risk. A stock gives a return to the investor by paying a dividend or by increasing in value and price. The concept has been around for a long time. Security Analysis by Benjamin Graham and David Dodd was first published in 1934. Revisions of the book are still in print. It is a simple concept. When a company earns money it has value. As earnings increase the value increases. The value of the stock is determined by an earnings multiplier. Earnings multipliers are dependent, among other things, than a rate of return. Risk.

As interest rates increase earnings multipliers decrease. For example a bank deposit gives me yield of 5%. So $1000 deposit would yield $50.

A comparable stock investment would pay a dividend of $50 and have a value of the same thousand dollars. However the stock has a degree of risk but it also has the ability to increase in price. So it may be worth more than one thousand dollars. It can also have decreased earnings. So it can be worth less a thousand dollars It has risk. What I am getting at is that stock multipliers are related to interest return. So that the total return on a stock is more or less than the return on a no risk fixed income investment. If earnings are going to go up it is worth more. If earnings go down it is worth less.

I cannot tell you at this time what price earnings multipliers should be because we don't know yet. We will know after stocks have been trading for some time and after we know what the returns are from other investments. It is my apparent that earnings multipliers are going to go down with higher interest rates. If for no other reason they must compete with no risk fixed income investments where the yield is increasing.

In the past we have had stocks selling and very high multiples. Some of them kind of crazy. Yes stock income can grow and the multiple that the stock sales for should reflect that. However we are seeing earnings multiples of 100 times, 50 time and so forth. In my opinion these are not going to be maintained in the future. What I am saying is the stocks will go down in price to provide a more reasonable earnings multiplier.

There are some classes of assets which are valued on a capitalization rate. This is very similar to valuing a stock at an earnings multiplier. I think the same parameters apply. I expect that capitalization rates will go up with interest rates. I think that this type of asset will go down in value.

At this time I think it is too early to say what earnings multiplier's for stocks and capitalization rates for other assets should be. With interest rates increasing to the point where better returns will be available on no risk deposits, it is very apparent that there will be downward adjustments to earnings.

Stated more simply if you receive a 5% return and from your bank account you would expect to have a higher rate of return from a stock investment. Otherwise there's no sense in buying stock. You can just put your money in the bank.

Is my opinion that we are going to go back to the type of earnings multipliers that we had in the

1980s when interest rates were high. I think that the days of stocks selling and 50 or 100 times earnings are gone.

That does not mean that we cannot get a high earnings multiplier. However, I think that they will be much less common than we see today.

It is probably going to take us two or three years to see what happens to stock multipliers. Think about it. It takes an enormous increase in earnings to justify an earnings multiplier of 25 times. That kind of multiplier was not uncommon a year or two ago.

This is further evidence that the conventional wisdom is not going to work. It will be interesting to see.

CHAPTER 17

INTEREST RATES INFLATION AND EMPLOYMENT

There is a well-established relationship in economic literature between interest rates, inflation and employment. This relationship is referred to as the Phillips curve in economic literature. I have mentioned this earlier in this book. The relationship is not complex. When interest rates increase economic activity is negatively affected. Employment then goes down. When the rate of unemployment goes up inflation goes down. The Fed is charged with maintaining stable prices and full employment. Those two parameters are in direct opposition.

The opposition between full employment and inflation has caused problems in the past when the Fed has raised interest rates. Therefore the Fed is somewhat in a box. They must juggle employment and inflation. If they tighten money too much they can get a desired result on inflation but it may be at the expense of employment. It is this opposition which has caused problems before for the Fed.

In this particular instance the situation is further complicated by the desire of the Fed to let a major portion of their portfolio run off. This operation will have an increased interest rate result. The question is what to do and how much.

Back in 1980, the Volcker recession, interest rates hit a high of 20%. Unemployment hit a high of 11%. We had a dozy of a recession. Not as bad as the 1930s, but it was a bad recession. The question is how far the Fed is going to go to raise interest rates. How much unemployment can they withstand?

There are two major differences this time. First we have started from a very low unemployment rate. Second we have started from very low interest rates and an economy that was doing well. The unknown factor in this mix is what the result will be. How much unemployment and what is acceptable.

There is also a side problem. As we increase interest rates the value of the US dollar increases relative to foreign currencies. This causes problems for other nations. That is another unknown that we have to cope with. The results of allowing federal debt on the Fed balance sheet to run off. This restricts, reduces, liquidity in the banking system. It also puts upward pressure on interest rates.

At this point in time I have no idea what the answer is. I also think that the Fed and the most knowledgeable economists have no idea either. We are just going to have to watch the situation and see what happens. I think that the controlling factor may be the rate of unemployment. I have no clue as to how high an unemployment rate is acceptable. 2023 is going to be an interesting year.

All of that taken into consideration the basic situation is that interest rates are going to increase. The stock market is going down. Where it ends we do not know yet.

CHAPTER 18

ECONOMIC SUMMERY

This book was written in September of 2022.

The purpose of this book is twofold. First I want to introduce you to a simple trend following investment system. Simple to use and it works. Second I want to make you aware that we are in the early stages of what will probably become a serious recession.

I expect that the Fed will continue to raise interest rates well into next year. We have already gotten a 3% increase from effectively a zero federal funds interest rates. I don't know how high interest rates will go but it is very apparent that they are headed considerably higher. We also have the second problem. Allowing the Treasury and agency debt on the Fed balance sheet to run off. This puts added pressure on increasing interest rates. We are in uncharted waters. We do not know the results of the proposed debt run off. It is the first time that we have seen this situation.

The other item that I want to make you aware of is that what I have been calling the conventional wisdom no longer works. The conventional wisdom basically says that the stock market will always correct itself in time, stocks continue to go up and you can expect a 6 to 10% return over time.

This conventional wisdom **does not work.** That is because it is the result of the easy money economy that we have had over the past 14 years. We are now in an environment of rapidly increasing interest rates. The world has changed! The conventional wisdom has not.

I have outlined the situation that the Fed is in. What they are doing. What their problems are. The unknowns in the current situation.

According to the conventional wisdom, if you are invested in stocks and have held on you are holding a sizable loss. It is my recommendation that at a minimum you go to cash. Neutral. Take your losses now. It will get worse as time goes on.

I have outlined my trading system. It is designed to follow the market and to protect you from taking sizable losses. The trading system is explained again in the next chapter along with various rules.

I have outlined the 1980 recession and made comparisons. It is very important for you to have some grounding and background in prior economic events.

I have given a brief explanation of where our current inflation comes from. It has nothing to do with the current administration. The present inflation has been building for over 10 years, it is the result of our economic policy since the 2008 banking crisis. Excess of liquidity and low interest rates are the reason for the inflation.

I expect that we will enter into a new era of price-to-earnings ratios based upon increased interest rates.

We can no longer expect that the stock market

will correct all transgressions. That the era of ultrahigh price earnings multipliers will return. It will not.

The good thing is that we can expect to once again receive a reasonable interest rate for our money deposited in a bank.

At some time in the future we can expect things I think that we are headed for a period of higher interest rates and higher unemployment. We also can expect to see the return of some rate of return on bank deposits. Interest rates to ease some and to get back to a more orderly world.

I cannot predict when this all will happen. I cannot predict how long the Fed will continue with its present policy. We will find out in time.

CHAPTER 19

VICTOR WEINTRAUB'S STOCK TRADING SYSTEN HOW IT WORKS ONCE AGAIN

This book outlines how my trading system works. It is very simple and almost anyone can do it with an hour a week at most once you have started. The trading system is a market following system. It does not employ armies of stock analysts to do all kinds of mumbo-jumbo to project the stock market and individual company earnings. We simply follow the market.

The first step is to determine the direction of the stock market. Up or down and by sectors. To do this we use Weintraub's Market Sector Analysis tool. This is my tool to determine the direction of the stock market based upon the 11GICS market sectors.

We also have specific rules. You must follow the rules to be successful.

Rule One: Never Fight the Fed. If the Fed is actively increasing interest rates the market is going to go down. We are going to have a recession. Only be on the **short** side of the market.

Rule Two: If there is an Interest Rate Inversion it means that we are going to have a recession. The market will go down. Only be on the **short** side of the market.

The second step is to pick stocks that are in an industry that is going up for long positions and an industry going down for a short positions. Pick stocks as instructed in chapter 9 and 10.

Rule Three: Only be long stocks in industries that are going up. Only be short stocks in industries that are going down.

Rule Four: If you are wrong on a stock selection and it is going against you, get rid of the stock.

Cut your losses. Do not hope for it to turn around. That is a long shot and the recipe for disaster.

Your next step is to have a balanced portfolio. That means if you have for example $100,000 to invest. Have 20 stocks in your portfolio. That means that no stock position is more than 5% of your portfolio. That way if you make a mistake you cannot get badly hurt.

You have to recognize that the people who present themselves to you as experts on the stock market are probably not. You also have to recognize that anybody who supports the conventional wisdom is misguided. The stock market does not always go up. The stock market does not always correct its errors given enough time. There is nothing wrong with selling a stock short. There is nothing wrong with holding cash.

As I have said earlier in this book, I do not recommend that investors use margin accounts to purchase stock. That is borrowing money and not investment. It is speculation.

A word about an investment plan such as a 401(k) or an IRA. If you are in that kind of a plan and you are in a down market you have a major problem. Your first alternative is to go to a self-directed plan. If that is not possible the only other alternative you have is to go to cash, a money market fund, to ride out a bear market and to minimize losses.

The objective of this book is to give you a basic rounding in economics. A little knowledge of what is happening in the real world can be of enormous value to you. It is always your objective to make money with your investments and not to be trapped into a situation where you have to take losses. You can always go to cash. There is no loss in cash and interest rates are going up. You should have a return on cash.

THE END

Made in the USA
Monee, IL
04 November 2026

67377015R00059